Creepy Sea Creatures

Written by Elizabeth Cook
Photography by Robert Yin

Published in the United States of America
by the Hameray Publishing Group, Inc.

Text © Elizabeth Cook
Published 2009

Publisher: Christine Yuen
Editorial Consultant: Adria Klein
Editor: Sara Sarver
Designer: Lois Stanfield

Photo credits: Robert Yin
Photos of the manta rays on pages 16, 17, and 18 are courtesy of Elizabeth Cook. Photo of the sea snake on page 34 is courtesy of Dave Hinkel.

Special thanks to the Scripps Institution of Oceanography for allowing access to their Marine Vertebrate Collection, for images on pages 4, 6, 8, 9, 10, and 11.

All rights reserved. No part of this publication may be reproduced or transmitted in any form or by any means without permission in writing from the publisher. Reproduction of any part of this book through photocopy, recording, or any electronic or mechanical retrieval system without the written permission of the publisher is an infringement of the copyright law.

ISBN 978-1-60559-101-8

Printed in Singapore

1 2 3 4 5 SIP 13 12 11 10 9

Contents

Chapter 1:	**Creepy Can Mean a Lot of Things**	5
Chapter 2:	**Monsters of the Deep**	7
Chapter 3:	**Just Plain Weird**	13
Chapter 4:	**Creeping Around the Reef**	23
Chapter 5:	**Jeepers, Creepers!**	35
Protecting Our Blue Planet		45
Fun Facts		46
Glossary		47
Index		48

CHAPTER 1

Creepy Can Mean a Lot of Things

The word "creepy" can describe many types of sea creatures. Some creepy sea creatures are dark, spooky monsters of the deep. Others are so strange, they are just plain weird. Then there are slow, slithery creatures that creep along the reef. Still other types of creepy sea creatures have sharp, shiny teeth. Seeing them can make the hair on the back of a person's neck stand up. Now that is creepy!

◀ This creature of the deep has scary-looking teeth.

CHAPTER 2

Monsters of the Deep

Some really creepy sea creatures live deep in the ocean. They have names such as fangtooth fish, black devil anglerfish, and viperfish. If these scary fish lived near the **surface** of the ocean, their spooky looks might keep people out of the water. But these fish all live so deep that no sun reaches where they live.

These scary fish have one other thing in **common**. Though creepy to look at, they are not likely to hurt people. After all, they are only six to twelve inches long.

◀ The fangtooth fish lives deep in the ocean.

▲ The fangtooth fish is named for its teeth. Its teeth are long like a cat's or dog's fangs.

Fangtooth Fish

Creepy **fang**-like teeth are what give the fangtooth fish its name. Its head is quite big and its tail is small. The fangtooth fish has a very wide mouth. This fish lives deep down in the dark ocean waters. Its home is more than fifteen hundred feet underwater.

The skin of the fangtooth fish is dark as well. Because of the dark water around it, other fish have trouble seeing the fangtooth fish. This means it can easily sneak up on **prey**. When a fish swims by not knowing the danger, the fangtooth fish uses its fang-like teeth to attack and kill.

◀ The black devil anglerfish has a fishing rod on its head. It uses the rod to draw fish close to its mouth.

Black Devil Anglerfish

The wicked-looking black devil anglerfish is another monster of the deep. As a creepy sea creature, it has a few special tricks. On the top of its head is a fleshy fishing rod. At the tip of this rod is a light that glows in the dark. In the dark waters of the deep ocean, the black devil anglerfish flicks on its light. A passing fish may stop and stare. Then the black devil anglerfish swiftly gobbles it down.

When the black devil anglerfish sucks a fish into its mouth, its teeth turn and point inward. That way, the trapped fish cannot escape.

The stomach of the black devil anglerfish is **bizarre** as well. It stretches and stretches like a balloon. The black devil anglerfish's stomach can hold a fish twice as big as its body.

◀ The viperfish has needle-like teeth that are too big to fit in its mouth.

Viperfish

The viperfish has a weird-looking head with an especially scary mouth. Its mouth is filled with needle-like teeth. The teeth look like the fangs of a viper, a deadly snake.

> The ocean gets darker the deeper one goes. That is because rays of sunlight cannot reach all the way to the bottom of the ocean. But the ocean is blue to about 450 feet. After that, the light grows dimmer until it is dark. At around 3,000 feet, the ocean is as dark as a moonless night.

The viperfish hunts in much the same way as the black devil anglerfish. The viperfish has a whip-like rod that sits behind its head. It bends that rod forward and dangles the tip in front of its mouth. At the tip of the rod is a light it turns off and on. When a fish swims by, it stares at the light. The **unwary** fish does not see the viperfish's creepy-looking mouth. Quickly, the viperfish snaps open its jaws. In one motion, its bottom jaw drops down and pushes forward. It scoops up the fish, and its viper-like teeth bite down.

▲ The viperfish has a large mouth and strong jaws to hold its prey. Its body is long and slender.

CHAPTER 3

Just Plain Weird

Some creepy sea creatures are just plain weird. Some have heads that look nothing like the head of a fish. There is a shark with a flat head. Its oddly shaped head comes in handy when it hunts. There is a special ray with horns on its head. Its horns are strange looking, but they help the animal eat. And finally, there is a fish that has hair on its body. Its hair helps it hide from other fish on the reef. Fish that look like these may not be very creepy, but they certainly are weird!

◀ Two ocean animals that have very strange heads are the hammerhead shark and the manta ray.

▲ The odd shape of the hammerhead shark's body and head makes the shark easy to recognize.

Hammerhead Sharks

When seen from above or below, the hammerhead shark has an unusual shape. Its head looks like the head of a hammer. Its body looks like the hammer's handle. Looking at the hammerhead shark this way, it is obvious why the animal got its name.

> Most sharks can smell quite well. They smell so well, in fact, that sharks are sometimes jokingly called swimming noses.

The hammerhead shark's weirdly shaped head is quite flat. Its head is also at least twice as wide as the head of most sharks. Its wide head has a large nose that sniffs out prey. This gives the hammerhead shark a good sense of smell. The hammerhead shark's large nose also makes it an excellent hunter. Once it finds its prey, it may use its "hammerhead" to pin the animal to the ocean floor.

Different types of hammerhead sharks are found throughout the world. Not all of them are large. Some grow to only three or four feet. But the great hammerhead shark, the biggest type of hammerhead shark, may grow to as much as fifteen feet long.

▲ The eyes of the hammerhead shark are at each end of its head.

Manta Rays

For many years, the manta ray was known as the devil ray. If viewed from above or below, the manta ray's head seems to have two devil-like horns. These two horns are actually flaps of skin rolled up like two flags. When unrolled, they are like big, flat hands or paddles. The manta ray uses these paddles to eat. It scoops tiny plants and animals known as plankton into its mouth. When the manta ray is swimming and not eating, it curls its paddles back up out of the way.

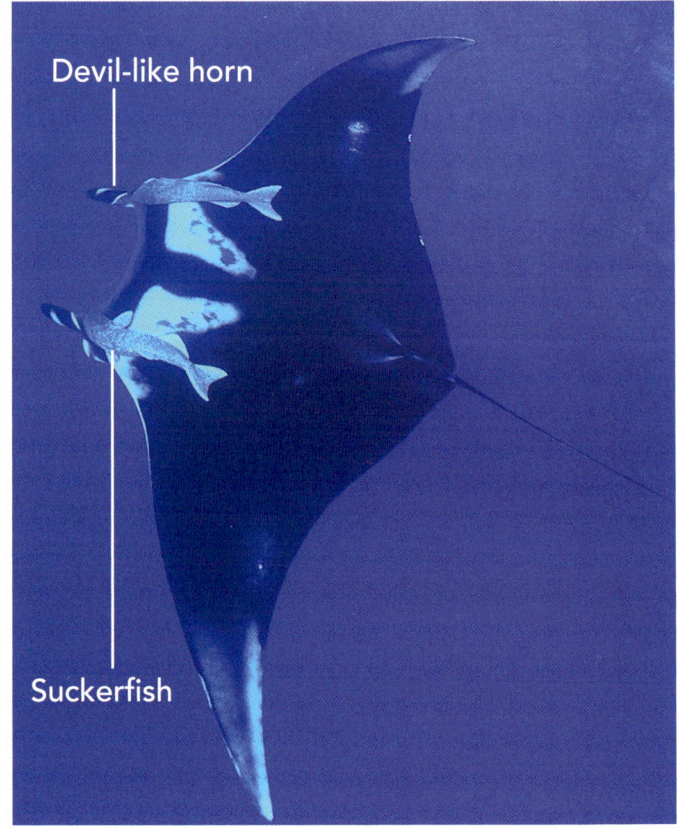

Suckerfish often attach themselves to manta rays and go for a ride. ▶

▲ The manta ray has two tightly curled-up horns at the front of its head.

All manta rays have the same shape. But each manta ray has a different pattern of colors and scars on its skin. Scientists often photograph the patterns and markings. These photographs help scientists track manta rays and learn more about them.

▲ When the manta ray eats, it unrolls its horns and uses these as paddles to scoop food into its mouth.

The manta ray does not deserve the creepy name devil ray. It is one of the most graceful animals in the ocean. Manta rays are not weird or dangerous to humans. But they are large animals that sometimes leap out of the water. Manta rays can be twelve feet wide. If a manta ray leaps out of the water and lands on someone, it could certainly hurt that person.

Scorpionfish

The scorpionfish is just plain weird as well as creepy looking. It seems to have hair all over its body. Actually, it is covered with skin flaps and **tassels**. Along with its ability to change color, its strange-looking "hair" helps it **blend** in with the reef.

▲ Scorpionfish can be quite beautiful.

Although scorpionfish may not all look alike, they all can sting with their spines. ▶

Like the wicked-looking land scorpion, the scorpionfish packs a sting. **Venom** is made in the **spines** in its back fin. A person who touches that fin will get a nasty surprise.

The scorpionfish is not a good swimmer. It prefers to sit in one place and blend in with the reef. For dinner, it waits until an unwary fish swims by. It suddenly opens its mouth as if it is yawning. Then it **slurps** the fish inside.

▲ The spines of the scorpionfish protect it from being bitten.

A FIRST-HAND ACCOUNT

On a dive in Indonesia, I hunted for the hard-to-find scorpionfish. Even though they come in bright colors, they blend in with the reef. I finally found one that was bright red. I crept nearer to get a good look at this weird fish. Just as I figured out where its eyes were, it surprised me. It opened its mouth and yawned. Since it did not seem bothered by me, it must have been time for its nap!

▲ Smart divers watch scorpionfish from a distance.

CHAPTER 4

Creeping Around the Reef

There are lots of ways to get around a reef. Fish swim, turtles glide, and crabs crawl. Some animals are fast, like the fastest shark. Some animals are slow, like the well-mannered sea turtle. But some of the slowest and most sluggish of all animals on the reef are sea cucumbers, sea anemones, and feather stars. When they move, they can only creep.

◀ Feather stars hold out their arms to catch tiny bits of food passing by.

▲ Female sea cucumbers raise their front ends to release eggs into the water.

Sea Cucumbers

Creeping slowly around the reef is an animal that looks like a very big **cucumber**. This ugly creature is called a sea cucumber. And, like a cucumber, it has no brain.

The sea cucumber has a long, chubby, worm-like body. When touched, its skin feels like leather. Its toothless mouth is on one end. Around its mouth are sticky, fleshy, finger-like tentacles. It sweeps food off the ocean floor with its tentacles. Then it curls each tentacle to its mouth and licks it clean.

The slow-creeping sea cucumber uses a couple of tricks to protect itself. If scared, it squirts water from both ends. If it is really scared, it spits its stomach out of its mouth. This captures the attention of its attacker while the sea cucumber moves away.

▲ A diver is lucky to see a sea cucumber releasing eggs.

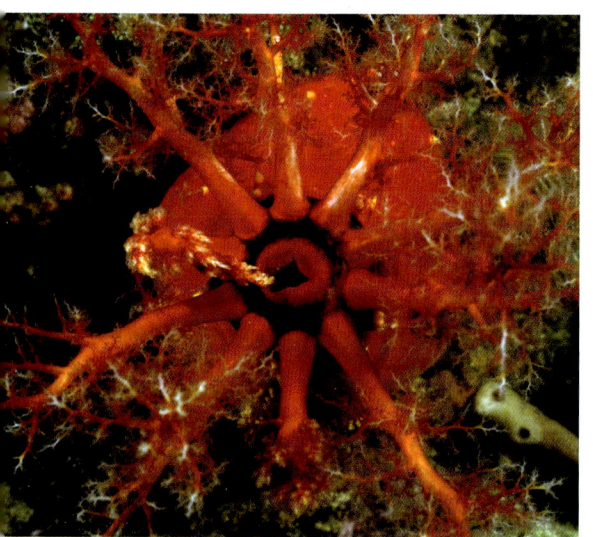 

▲ Sea cucumbers open their tentacles wide to gather bits of food.

Sea cucumbers can be different colors. They can be red, brown, or yellow. Some have unusual patterns. Others have strange but pretty skin flaps that look like shaggy hair. Sea cucumbers use tiny, tube-shaped feet to pull themselves along the ocean floor.

> In some areas of the world, sea cucumbers are gathered from the ocean floor. Then they are dried and sold for medicine and food. Some people who are sick believe that eating sea cucumbers helps them heal quickly. Sea cucumbers are served in soup and other dishes.

▲ Sea cucumbers creep across the ocean floor looking for food.

A person who looks closely at a sea cucumber may find a surprise. Tiny crabs and sea stars often ride along on the sea cucumber. Another strange animal that lives with the sea cucumber is the pearlfish. This fish makes its home inside the sea cucumber's body. When hungry, it nibbles chunks out of the poor sea cucumber's insides. Now that is a creepy sea creature!

Sea Anemones

Sea anemones spend much of their time attached to the reef. When spread wide open, they look like underwater flowers. But smart fish know to stay away. The sea anemone's flowing fingers are actually deadly tentacles. When the right size of fish or animal comes near, the pretty flower reaches out with its tentacles to sting and **stun** it. The creepy sea anemone can even kill and eat a sea star.

▲ Sea anemones look like ocean flowers. But they can move from place to place on the ocean floor.

This sea anemone has been eating a blue sea star. ▶

The sea anemone has a mouth in the center of its body. Its tentacles pass food to its mouth. ▶

Like some jellyfish, the sea anemone gives a powerful sting. Sea anemones can be found in all sorts of colors, including blue, green, and red. Some even have stripes. Sometimes sea anemones are only an inch wide. Others grow to six feet wide.

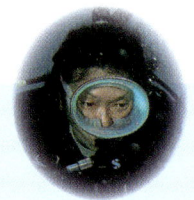

A FIRST-HAND ACCOUNT

On many dives, I had seen beautiful, flower-like sea anemones. They always looked lovely and harmless. Their tentacles waved gently in the ocean water. Often I would see clownfish and shrimp hiding in the tentacles of a sea anemone. But I knew that the sea anemone was not always friendly to fish.

One afternoon dive, I spotted a bright red squirrelfish. It looked odd because it could not move. I realized that it was trapped in the tentacles of a sea anemone. The tentacles were pulling the fish into the anemone's mouth. I pulled on the fish's tail to free it from the grip of the creepy sea anemone. Once free, the fish held still for a moment. Then it shot out of sight. Suddenly, I felt bad for taking the meal right out of the sea anemone's mouth!

The flower-like sea anemone can catch and eat large fish. ▶

▲ Feather stars often climb onto the fingers of soft coral to catch food as it drifts by.

Feather Stars

The feather star looks much like a **cluster** of feathers. This animal comes in many different colors. It can be orange, gold, red, blue, or green, as well as black and white. Some feather stars even have two colors on their arms.

▲ The feather star walks from place to place on the reef on thin little legs.

The feather star also looks like a plant. In fact, it looks so much like a plant that it is often called a sea lily. But the feather star has arms that can be ten or more inches long. These feather-like arms rise upward and reach outward from around its mouth.

Most of the day, the feather star can be hard to find. It hides in cracks along the reef. But at night, using claw-like legs, this creepy sea creature climbs out of the crack and creeps along the reef. In the safety of the dark, it spreads its arms wide open. With its sticky arms, it catches tiny bits of food passing by. The arms then pass the food down to the feather star's mouth.

Sticky arms

▲ A feather star reaches out to touch the diver's mask.

The plant-like arms of the feather star stretch out to touch and feed. ▶

CHAPTER 5

Jeepers, Creepers!

Some things just give a person "the creeps." Things that slither are rather creepy. Things with sharp, pointy teeth are pretty creepy, too. Then there are things that just look plain scary—things people do not want to touch. And certainly there are things people would not want to have hooked to their bodies.

But, creepy or not, ocean animals that slither or look really scary are interesting to learn about. Divers come across these creepy sea creatures every day.

◄ Sleek sea snakes are among the creepiest animals in the ocean.

Barracudas

The barracuda is a long, sleek fish. It has a silvery body that looks fast and powerful. The barracuda is certainly very strong. But most of the time it just hangs in the water. It seems not to want to go anywhere. Its very black eyes watch everything carefully. That dark, **steady** stare gives people the creeps. The barracuda looks ready to pounce if the right fish swims by.

▲ Divers find the steady stare of the barracuda to be pretty creepy.

▲ The largest type of barracuda is known as the great barracuda. It usually hunts alone.

The barracuda has fierce-looking teeth. Its teeth are designed to bite down on fish. But the barracuda is harmless to people. A barracuda can eat a big fish with no problem. Still, it seems not to be interested in anything the size of a person. Perhaps people give the barracuda the creeps?

Whitetip Reef Sharks

Whitetip reef sharks hide in caves or under ledges during the day. At night, they swim out and chase prey into cracks in the reef. Then they pin down their prey and use their pointed teeth to kill and eat it.

Whitetip reef sharks are shy. If a diver tries to go near them, they usually move away. But coming nose to nose with large sharks resting in a cave could make even the bravest of divers shout, "Jeepers, creepers!"

▲   Whitetip reef sharks are often found in caves.

▲ This strange-looking worm can eat small fish.

Giant Worms

Giant worms known as Bobbit worms hide in the sand during the day. These worms can grow as long as ten feet. At night, they lift their heads out of the sand to hunt. The jaws and mouths of these creepy worms are wider than their bodies. Hooks on their jaws help grab small fish that pass by. Their jaws are so strong that they can slice a fish in half in one fast bite. Then, in less than a second, they disappear under the sand with their dinner.

▲ Sea snakes are shy and afraid of divers.

Sea Snakes

People who like snakes would find sea snakes to be handsome animals. But most people think sea snakes are creepy sea creatures. Sea snakes are different from land snakes. Their tails are flat on the end. This makes a good paddle that they use to help them swim. It is interesting that a snake can swim at all. Sea snakes do have to go to the surface to breathe. And some, but not all, types of sea snakes go on land to lay eggs.

▲ Sea snakes slither across the reef or swim through open water.

◀ Sea snakes flick their tongues like many land snakes.

Sea snakes hunt for small fish. They have a quick way of killing their prey. They use sharp fangs for grabbing and stabbing. When a sea snake catches a fish, its fangs punch holes in the fish. Venom spurts through the fangs into the fish. The fish dies very quickly. Then the sea snake swallows its dinner without the fish fighting back.

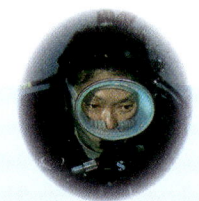

A FIRST-HAND ACCOUNT

Not long ago, I spent a week diving in Indonesia. I wanted so much to see a deadly sea snake before the end of the trip. I hoped that I would be able to take this animal's picture.

On the very last dive, I searched really hard for the shy sea snake. I paused and placed my right hand on a piece of dead **coral**. To my left, I watched a school of fish. Suddenly, I felt something slithering around my left wrist. I looked down to see a sea snake snaking its way toward my face. I do not know which of us was more scared. Upon seeing my eyes, the shy sea snake spun off my arm and sped away.

▲ Careful divers do not get too close to sea snakes.

▲ The spotted sweetlips fish is often a home for the creepy isopod.

Isopods

Isopods are just plain scary. Some types of isopods attach themselves to the head of a fish, often near the eyes. Once attached, they stay on the fish forever.

Some of these isopods are no trouble at all to a fish. They are just along for the ride. They latch on with fourteen hook-like legs. Then they feed on small bits of food that float through the water.

But other types of isopods are not so kind. They crawl inside the fish's gills or drill holes in its flesh. These isopods are parasites. They eat the fish's flesh and blood. Parasite or not, it is hard to call an animal that lives its life hooked on another animal anything but creepy.

Protecting Our Blue Planet

Ways We Can Help

- The bottom of the ocean may seem a long way down. But ocean animals can be harmed by what people drop in the ocean or in rivers, which flow into the ocean. Never throw trash of any kind into rivers, lakes, or the ocean.

- Read the labels on household cleaning, gardening, and automobile products to learn how to throw them away the right way. The contents of these cans and containers can end up in the ocean.

- Take a **submarine** trip and learn more about creatures of the deep at: http://www.seasky.org/deep-sea/introduction.html.

- To learn more about how deep scientists and ocean animals have been, visit this Web site: http://seawifs.gsfc.nasa.gov/OCEAN_PLANET/HTML/education_diving_records.html.

- To learn more about creepy sea creatures, visit this Web site: http://www.extremescience.com/deepcreat.htm. Then share the Web site with a friend and talk about the sea creatures.

◀ A field of colorful feather stars covers this part of the reef.

Fun Facts

If deep-sea fish live so deep in the ocean, how is anything known about them?
For many years, scientists did not have many ways to study fish found deep in the ocean. They used large nets known as trawls. Trawls were dragged across the bottom of the ocean. Fish and other ocean animals were caught in the big nets. Then they were pulled up to the surface. Most animals were dead by the time they reached the surface. Studying dead animals was helpful, but did not answer the many questions scientists had.

    Today, much better tools are used. Scientists can use small submarines to take pictures of animals deep underwater and to study their **behavior**. There are also new traps that bring deep ocean animals to the surface still alive. All these tools have helped scientists to find out a lot more about what lives deep in the sea.

What do hammerhead sharks eat?
There are different types of hammerhead sharks. Not all of them eat the same thing. Most of them eat a diet of fish such as sardines and jacks. Some like octopus and squid. The largest of the hammerhead sharks, the great hammerhead shark, and the slightly smaller smooth hammerhead shark both eat stingrays. They also eat smaller sharks.

Do manta rays have stingers on their tails?
Manta rays do not have stingers as other rays do. It is safe to swim or dive with manta rays. But manta rays do weigh a lot and could hurt someone with a strong flap of a wing tip. So it is important not to get too close to manta rays.

Do all manta rays look alike?
Scientists have discovered that manta rays in different parts of the world have different patterns. For example, manta rays in the eastern part of the Pacific Ocean are mostly dark underneath. But manta rays found in the western part of the Pacific Ocean are usually white underneath.

Glossary

behavior	The way an animal acts
bizarre	Strange or unusual
blend	To match or look somewhat like something else
cluster	Group or bunch
common	The same as or similar to something
coral	Tiny animals that live together in large groups or colonies; the bodies of dead corals turn into coral reefs
cucumber	A long green vegetable that is often sliced and served in a salad
fang	A sharp tooth used to pierce skin
prey	Animals that are hunted and eaten by another animal
slurps	Sucks in noisily
spines	Long, thin, sharp body parts that ocean animals use to protect themselves
steady	Fixed or motionless
stun	To make unable to move for a few minutes
submarine	A boat that can go completely underwater
surface	The top of a body of water
tassels	Dangling pieces that look like threads of yarn tied together
unwary	Not careful
venom	A poison that is delivered by a bite or a sting

Index

arms, 23, 31–33
attach, 16, 28, 43
attack, 8

barracuda, 36–37
behavior, 46
bite, 11, 37, 39
bizarre, 9
black devil anglerfish, 7, 9, 11
blend, 19–21
Bobbit worm, 39
body, 9, 11, 13, 14, 19, 24, 27, 29, 36, 39
brain, 24
breathe, 40

clownfish, 30
cluster, 31
color, 17, 19, 21, 26, 29, 31
common, 7
coral, 31, 42
crab, 27
cucumber, 24

devil ray, 16, 18 (see also manta ray)
diver, 21, 25, 33, 35, 36, 38, 40, 42

eat, 13, 16, 18, 24, 28, 30, 33, 37, 38, 39, 43, 46
eggs, 24, 25, 40
eyes, 15, 21, 36, 43

fang, 8, 10, 41
fangtooth fish, 7–8
feather star, 23, 31–33, 45
feet, 26
fin, 20

gills, 43
glows in the dark, 9

great barracuda, 37
great hammerhead shark, 15, 46

hair, 13, 19
hammerhead shark, 13, 14–15, 46
head, 8, 9, 10, 11, 13, 14–15, 16, 17, 39, 43
hide, 13, 33, 38, 39
hook, 39, 43
horns, 13, 16, 17, 18
hunt, 11, 13, 37, 39, 41

isopod, 43

jaws, 11, 39
jellyfish, 29

legs, 32–33, 43

manta ray, 13, 16–18, 46
markings, 17
mouth, 8, 9, 10, 11, 16, 18, 20, 24–25, 29, 30, 32–33, 39

nose, 15

Pacific Ocean, 46
paddles, 16, 18, 40
parasite, 43
pattern, 17, 26, 46
pearlfish, 27
plankton, 16
prey, 8, 11, 15, 38, 41

reef, 5, 13, 19, 20, 21, 23, 24, 28, 32, 33, 38, 41, 45
ride, 16, 27, 43
rod, 9, 11

school, 42

scientist, 17, 45, 46
scorpionfish, 19–21
sea anemone, 23, 28–30
sea cucumber, 23, 24–27
sea lily, 32
sea snake, 35, 40–42
sea star, 27, 28
shape, 14, 17
shark, 13–15, 38, 46
skin, 8, 17, 24
skin flap, 19, 26
slurps, 20
smell, 14, 15
smooth hammerhead shark, 46
spines, 19, 20
squirrelfish, 30
sting, 19, 20, 28–29
stinger, 46
stomach, 9, 25
stun, 28
submarine, 45, 46
suckerfish, 16
sunlight, 10
surface, 7, 40, 46
sweetlips, 43
swim, 16, 40, 41, 46

tail, 8, 40, 46
tassels, 19
teeth, 5, 8, 9, 10, 11, 35, 37, 38
tentacles, 24, 26, 28, 29, 30
tongue, 41
trap, 46
trawl, 46

venom, 20, 41
viperfish, 7, 10–11

whitetip reef shark, 38
worm, 39